SCHOLASTIC

GRADES 4–6

Reading Response Trifolds for 40 Popular Nonfiction Books

by Jennifer Cerra-Johansson

New York • Toronto • London • Auckland • Sydney
Mexico City • New Delhi • Hong Kong • Buenos Aires

Teaching *Resources*

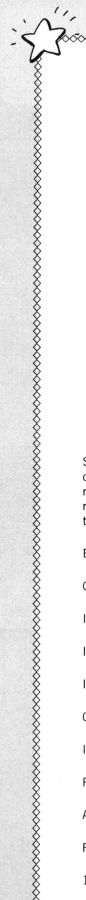

For Martin

Scholastic Inc. grants teachers permission to photocopy the reproducible pages from this book for classroom use. No other part of this publication may be reproduced in whole or in part, or stored in a retrieval system, or transmitted in any form or by any means, electronic, mechanical, photocopying, recording, or otherwise, without permission of the publisher. For information regarding permission, write to Scholastic Inc., 557 Broadway, New York, NY 10012

Edited by Mela Ottaiano

Cover design by Scott Davis

Interior design by Melinda Belter

Illustrations by Teresa Anderko

ISBN: 978-0-545-44878-9

Copyright © 2014 by Jennifer Cerra-Johansson

Illustrations copyright © 2014 by Scholastic Inc.

Published by Scholastic Inc.

Printed in the U.S.A.

1 2 3 4 5 6 7 8 9 10   40   21 20 19 18 17 16 15 14

Contents

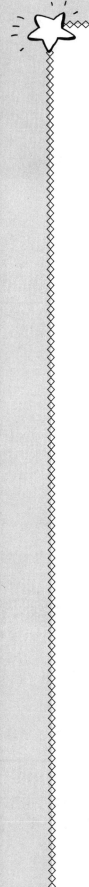

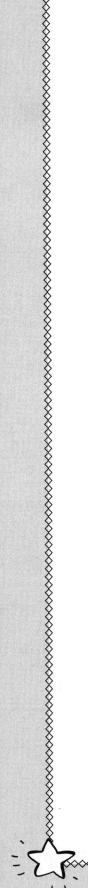

Introduction

Throughout my years as an elementary school teacher, nonfiction has always held a special place in my heart. Often my most reluctant readers are drawn to nonfiction and, through it, I am able to hook all students on the world of reading. The challenging part is helping children navigate their way through complex ideas and tricky vocabulary. I can best help students by first reading the book myself and identifying the most challenging parts. Next, I choose which reading strategies and text features will support comprehension and use these to create reading response trifolds.

Even though nonfiction books at these grade levels aren't necessarily very long, this process can still be time consuming. During this process, I keep in mind the importance of helping my students purposefully read and remain focused. I also want to hold them accountable for what they read and be able to easily assess their understanding and progress— while I have several groups reading different books simultaneously. To help accomplish all of this, I create and use reading response trifolds specific to each nonfiction book as part of my small-group instruction.

What Are Reading Response Trifolds?

Reading response trifolds are activity sheets that students refer to and interact with during each guided reading session. Students can also use the folded sheet as a convenient bookmark.

Each trifold includes a pre-reading section, Get Ready to Read, which guides students to preview the book and think about the topic and what they might already know about it. This section also

Connections to the COMMON CORE

Since the trifolds included in this book were created with the Common Core State Standards in mind, they address the following English Language Arts standards:

RI.4.1	RI.5.1	RI.6.1
RI.4.2	RI.5.2	RI.6.2
RI.4.3	RI.5.3	RI.6.3
RI.4.4	RI.5.4	RI.6.4
RI.4.5	RI.5.5	RI.6.5
RI.4.6	RI.5.6	RI.6.6
RI.4.7	RI.5.7	RI.6.7
RI.4.8	RI.5.8	RI.6.8
RI.4.9	RI.5.9	RI.6.9
RI.4.10	RI.5.10	RI.6.10

For more details about these standards, visit: www.core standards.org/ELA-Literacy points out specific text features, such as headings, diagrams, pronunciation keys, or captions that will help students understand what they are reading.

The central sections of most trifolds contain three parts: Strategy, Focus, and Respond. The Strategy component helps students review a specific reading comprehension strategy, such as find the main idea, compare and contrast, use context clues, or summarize. Next, students read the Focus section, where they are given a purpose for reading a specific section of the text. After students have finished reading, they answer the Respond question. This requires them to refer back to the reading and apply the specific reading strategy to help them formulate a response. I ask students to cite information directly from the text to support their thinking, which is an important requirement of the Common Core State Standards (CCSS) for reading informational text.

In the final section of each trifold, students have the opportunity to extend their learning.

TIP According to Fountas and Pinnell's guided-reading text gradient, fourth graders typically read between levels O–T, fifth graders read between levels S–W, and sixth graders range from level V–Z. The decoding skills of students at these grade levels are advanced enough that more emphasis can be placed on higher-level reading strategies and responses. We included books through level W to provide material for more advanced sixth grade readers.

Trifolds in Action

Using trifolds as part of my small-group instruction has proven to be an effective way to teach and reinforce reading strategies. To introduce or review a particular section's reading strategy I begin by asking students to tell me what they know or remember about the strategy. I proceed to a think-aloud, where I read from a text, apply the strategy, and share my thought process aloud. This model provides students with an internal dialogue they can apply when reading independently.

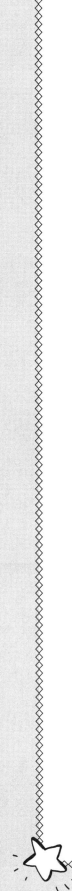

You might say the following when doing a think-aloud for each strategy:

Preview

• I notice _____ .

• I already know _____ .

• I want to find out _____ .

Find the Main Idea

• The big idea is _____ .

• This is mostly about _____ .

Identify Key Details

• What details support the main topic or idea?

• It's important that _____ .

• I want to remember _____ .

Compare and Contrast

• How is _____ similar to _____ ?

• How is _____ different from _____ ?

• They are the same or different because _____ .

Analyze Cause and Effect

• _____ happened because of _____ .

• _____ led to _____ .

• If _____ didn't happen, then _____ .

Question

- Why _____ ?

- How come _____ ?

- I wonder _____ .

Determine Importance

- I know this is important because _____ .

- _____ is interesting, but _____ is important because _____ .

- This text feature shows me that _____ is important.

- This part answered the question _____ .

Use Context Clues

- What word would make sense here?

- Is there a part of this word I've seen before?

- The pictures helped me figure out that _____ .

- The next sentence says _____ so I think this might mean _____ .

Make Inferences

- Maybe this means _____ .

- I think this happened because _____ .

- This part makes me think _____ .

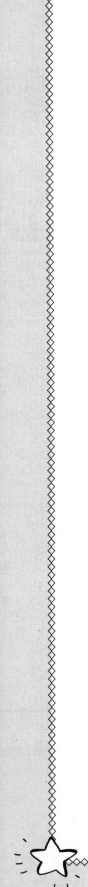

Categorize

• How does this information fit together?

• I notice _____ and _____ go together because _____ .

Identify Author's Purpose

• The author wants me to learn _____ .

• I believe the author feels _____ because _____ .

• I think the author wrote this book to show _____ .

Evaluate

• When I read this part, it made me feel _____ .

• My opinion is _____ .

• I think _____ because _____ .

Synthesize

• Before I thought _____ , but now I know _____ .

• Now I understand that _____ .

• Oh! I get it that _____ .

Summarize

• First _____ , then _____ . After that, _____ . Finally, _____ .

• The most important parts were _____ .

After going over a reading strategy, I continue by previewing the Focus element in the same section. Students then read a small amount of the text, keeping that focal point in mind. In most cases, students must use sticky notes to mark important information as they read, increasing their interaction with the text. While all students are reading silently, I spend a few minutes with individual students listening to them read aloud. This enables me to help students improve their fluency, expression, and decoding skills.

 Refer to the bibliography on page 95 to identify the editions that were used to create these trifold assignments. If you are using a different edition than the one in the bibliography, please preview the trifold before distributing it to students in case the page number assignments are slightly off. You should only need a quick scan of the material to make any necessary revisions. If you do need to revise the page numbers, you may want to photocopy one trifold first. Then you can use correcting liquid to cover the old page numbers and write in those that match the edition you are using.

Once students have finished reading the entire section, they answer the Respond section independently. Then, they share their responses with the group. As they do so, I can assess their understanding of the material. This process also helps students work through any confusion on the spot. When students return a book, I ask them to peel off any sticky notes, write their name on the notes, and hand them in. I use these notes as ongoing assessment to inform future instruction.

The trifolds serve as both an instructional tool and a management technique. With four or five different guided reading groups generally going in my classroom, we are using four or five different books each day. Remembering specific book elements and which strategies would best suit a section of text can be challenging without a system in place. Preparing these trifolds ahead of time consistently helps my guided reading groups run smoothly and efficiently. Using them has enabled me to meet the diverse needs of my students. Children love guided reading time because they have an opportunity to read quality informational texts at their instructional reading levels, interact more deeply with the text, and communicate their thoughts with the teacher.

Using trifolds in the context of guided reading offers students a smooth transition to using them during independent reading—enhancing their experience and developing a joy of reading.

How to Assemble a Trifold

To assemble the reading response trifolds so they appear back-to-back as they do in the book, you'll need access to a copier that makes double-sided copies. Then, follow these easy steps:

1. Photocopy both trifold pages, single-sided. (See figure 1.)

2. Place the page with the title panel, section 4, and section 5 (side A) on top of the page with sections 1, 2, and 3 (side B). (See figure 2.)

3. Feed this through a photocopier set to create one double-sided page from two single-sided pages.

4. Distribute a trifold sheet to each student.

5. Direct students to fold the panels so that the title page ends up on top, similar to a brochure. (See figure 3.)

6. Finally, students should follow the directions on each of the panels to complete the reading response trifolds. If students find they need more room to write or to illustrate, they can use a separate piece of paper and attach it to the trifold with a stapler.

Side A

Side B

figure 1

Side B   Side A

figure 2

figure 3

TIP

If you don't have access to a copier that makes double-sided copies, you can glue or staple the pages back to back before distributing them to students. (See figures 4 and 5.) Then students can continue directly to steps 5 and 6.

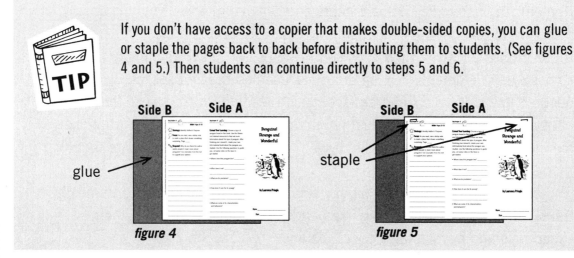

Side B   Side A

glue

figure 4

Side B   Side A

staple

figure 5

Cats vs. Dogs

by Elizabeth Carney

Name _____

Date _____

Extend Your Learning: Write a persuasive letter to a parent asking for a cat or dog. Use the information in this book to support your point of view.

_____
_____
_____
_____
_____
_____
_____
_____
_____
_____
_____

READ: Pages 28–45

Strategy: Summarize

Focus: As you read, use the bold red headings to help you focus on the big ideas in the last seven sections. Write a one-sentence summary on a sticky note after reading each section.

Respond: Use your sticky notes to help you write a brief summary of each chapter below.

"Behavior"	
"Final Showdown"	

GET READY TO READ

☆ **Strategy:** Preview

💡 **Think:** Which animal do you already like best: cats or dogs? Why?

_____

_____

_____

Text Feature Focus: This book contains many helpful text features, such as a table of contents, glossary, index, photos, captions, pronunciation keys, and bold headings. These features will help you understand difficult ideas in the text. Be sure to take your time and use the visual information as you read each section.

READ: Pages 4–13

☆ **Strategy:** Compare and Contrast

🔍 **Focus:** As you read, use a sticky note to mark a similarity cats and dogs share.

Page _____

Explain.

_____

_____

✏️ **Respond:** How are cats' and dogs' senses different?

_____

_____

_____

_____

_____

_____

READ: Pages 14–27

☆ **Strategy:** Make Inferences

🔍 **Focus:** As you read, use a sticky note to mark a place that shows how dogs can express feelings through their actions.

Page _____

Explain.

_____

_____

✏️ **Respond:** What can you infer from a hissing cat?

_____

_____

_____

_____

_____

_____

Constellations

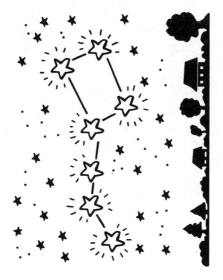

by Diane M. Sipiera
and Paul P. Sipiera

Name _____

Date _____

SECTION 5

Extend Your Learning: For thousands of years, humans have used their imaginations to create constellations. Choose a well-known constellation. In the space below, draw the stars found in that constellation. Then, on another sheet of paper, make up your own constellation for that group of stars, draw it, and name your new creation.

SECTION 4

READ: Pages 33–43

Strategy: Evaluate

Focus: As you read, use sticky notes to mark the constellations you would most like to see in the night sky.

Pages _____

Respond: Why do you think humans have been interested in stars throughout time?

GET READY TO READ

Think: What do you already know about constellations?

_____

_____

_____

Strategy: Preview

Text Feature Focus: This book contains many text features, such as photos and illustrations with captions, chapters with titles, and a glossary of important words. These features will help you understand difficult ideas in the text. Before reading each chapter, use the title to help you think about what you will learn in that section.

READ: Pages 5–16

Strategy: Find the Main Idea

Focus: As you read, use the chapter titles to predict what you will learn about in each chapter. Then use the titles to help you focus on the main idea of each chapter.

Respond: Record the main idea of each chapter you read.

| The Origins of Constellations | |
| What Are Constellations? | |

READ: Pages 17–32

Strategy: Summarize

Focus: As you read, stop at the end of each section and record the most important ideas on a sticky note.

Respond: After reading both chapters, use your sticky notes to help you write a few sentences summarizing what you learned.

_____

_____

_____

_____

_____

_____

_____

_____

_____

Endangered Animals

by Lynn M. Stone

Name _____

Date _____

SECTION 5

Extend Your Learning: Turn to the Index on pages 46–48. Choose an animal you would like to learn more about. Use the library and Internet resources to learn about the animal and what people can do to protect it.

Write some notes on the lines to get started. Then, write your own nonfiction book about the animal you investigated.

Notes: _____

_____

_____

_____

_____

_____

_____

_____

_____

_____

_____

SECTION 4

READ: Pages 28–44

Strategy: Identify Author's Purpose

Focus: As you read, record three ways people can help endangered animals.

1. _____

2. _____

3. _____

Respond: Why do you think the author wrote this book?

_____

_____

_____

_____

_____

_____

_____

_____

_____

SECTION 1

Strategy: Preview

Think: After previewing the Table of Contents, record a question you have about this topic.

_____

_____

_____

Text Feature Focus: This book contains many text features, such as photos with captions, chapter titles, and a glossary with pronunciation key. These features will help you understand difficult ideas in the text. Be sure to take your time and use the visual information as you read each section.

SECTION 2

Strategy: Analyze Cause and Effect

Focus: As you read, record some of the ways humans have caused animals to become endangered.

_____

_____

_____

Respond: What effect did humans poisoning prairie dogs have on the black-footed ferret?

_____

_____

_____

_____

_____

SECTION 3

Strategy: Find the Main Idea

Focus: As you read, record three important details in the chart below.

Page	Important Details

Respond: What is the main idea of this section?

_____

_____

_____

_____

_____

Rocks and Minerals

by Ann O. Squire

Name _____

Date _____

Strategy: Evaluate

Focus: As you read, use a sticky note to mark a place that suprises you.
Page _____

Respond: Describe how rocks and minerals are important in today's modern world.

_____
_____
_____
_____
_____
_____
_____

Extend Your Learning: How have people used rocks throughout history? On another sheet of paper, create a web showing how humans have used rocks throughout time. Use the following categories: prehistoric humans, Native Americans, ancient Romans, and modern humans.

Strategy: Categorize

Focus: As you read, record the three types of rocks.

1. _____

2. _____

3. _____

Respond: Complete the chart with the name of each type of rock listed above. Then describe how the rocks are formed.

Rock Type	How is it formed?	

GET READY TO READ

Strategy: Preview

Think: After previewing the Table of Contents, record something you will learn from reading this book.

Text Feature Focus: This book contains many text features, such as photos and illustrations with captions, chapters with titles, and a glossary of important words. These features will help you understand difficult ideas in the text. Look at the pictures and captions before reading each page.

TIP

When previewing the book, take a look at page 43 to find out about meteorites. Why do you think meteorites are included in a book about rocks and minerals?

READ: Pages 5–13

Strategy: Synthesize

Focus: As you read, record what each layer of Earth is made of in the chart below.

Crust	
Mantle	
Outer Core	
Inner Core	

Respond: Describe how rocks and minerals combine to make Earth.

READ: Pages 14–21

Strategy: Identify Key Details

Focus: As you read, record three important details about minerals in the chart below.

Page	Important Details

Respond: Use the information above to help you answer the chapter title "What are minerals?"

Heroes of the Revolution

by David A. Adler

Name _____

Date _____

Extend Your Learning: Read the Important Dates timeline on pages 29–30. Choose an event you would like to learn more about. Use Internet resources and the library to help you with your research. Before beginning your research, write a list of questions you would like to answer.

My Questions:

1. _____

2. _____

3. _____

4. _____

5. _____

6. _____

READ: Pages 20–27

⭐ **Strategy:** Analyze Cause and Effect

🔍 **Focus:** As you read, look for each hero's important action and its effect.

✏️ **Respond:** Record each hero's important action and its effect.

Hero	Action	Effect
Paul Revere		
Haym Salomon		
Deborah Sampson		
George Washington		

GET READY TO READ

⭐ **Strategy:** Preview

💡 **Think:** What does the word *hero* mean to you?

_____

_____

↘ **Text Feature Focus:** This book includes brief profiles of 12 heroes who lived during the American Revolution. Each profile includes an illustration depicting the heroic act and the hero's date of birth and death. Be sure to preview the illustrations carefully to help you make predictions about what you will learn.

READ: Pages 5–11

⭐ **Strategy:** Find the Main Idea

🔍 **Focus:** As you read, stop at the end of each profile and ask yourself, *How is this person a hero?*

✏ **Respond:** Record your ideas below.

Hero	How is this person a hero?
Ethan Allen	
Crispus Attucks	
Lydia Darragh	
Nathan Hale	

READ: Pages 12–19

⭐ **Strategy:** Make Inferences

🔍 **Focus:** As you read, stop at the end of each profile and record a word that describes the hero.

✏ **Respond:** Cite evidence from the text to support the word you recorded to describe each hero.

Hero	Word	Evidence From the Text
Mary Hays		
Thomas Jefferson		
John Paul Jones		
Thomas Paine		

Stargazers

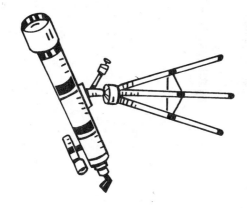

by Gail Gibbons

Name _____

Date _____

Extend Your Learning: Choose one of the events described in the timeline on page 31 that you would like to learn more about. Use Internet resources and the library to help you with your research.

Jot some notes on the lines to get started. Then, write a report on another sheet of paper.

Notes: _____

_____

_____

_____

_____

_____

_____

_____

_____

_____

Strategy: Summarize

Focus: As you read, think about these 5 Ws (and an H) to help you remember important ideas from the text.

What tools can stargazers use to help them see stars?

Why do they need these tools?

How are refracting and reflecting telescopes different?

Who uses observatories to study the sky?

Where can people go to learn about stars?

When was the first telescope invented?

 Respond: Use the information you thought about above to help you write a few sentences summarizing what you read.

_____

_____

_____

_____

_____

GET READY TO READ

Strategy: Preview

Think: What do you already know about stars?

_____

_____

_____

_____

⇨ **Text Feature Focus:** This book contains many text features, such as illustrations with captions, diagrams, and a timeline. These features will help you understand difficult ideas in the text. Be sure to take your time and use the visual information to help you navigate each section.

Strategy: Synthesize

Focus: As you read, record the information you learn about stars in the chart below.

Red Stars	
Yellow Stars	
White Stars	
"Twinkling" Stars	

Respond: The sun is eight light minutes from us. How far away from Earth is the next nearest star?

_____

_____

_____

Strategy: Find the Main Idea

Focus: As you read, record three important details in the chart below.

Page	Important Details	

Respond: What is the main idea of this section?

_____

_____

_____

Who Would Win?
Killer Whale
vs.
Great White Shark

by Jerry Pallotta

Name _____

Date _____

SECTION 5

Extend Your Learning: How do you think the story should have ended? Rewrite your own ending.

_____
_____
_____
_____
_____
_____
_____
_____
_____
_____

SECTION 4

READ: Pages 24–32

⭐ **Strategy:** Find the Main Idea

🔍 **Focus:** As you read, record which animal wins.

Winner: _____

✏️ **Respond:** Why does this animal win? What are its advantages?

_____
_____
_____
_____
_____
_____
_____
_____
_____

Strategy: Preview

Think: Look at the animals on the cover. Predict which animal you think will win.

Prediction:

Text Feature Focus: Throughout the book, the author uses many text features, such as illustrations, photos, diagrams, and geometrical graphics, to call attention to special facts and definitions. Be sure to stop and read these important parts.

•••••••••• TIP ••••••••••

When previewing a book, pay attention to its text structure. In this book, every two pages the author describes one characteristic. The information about the killer whale is always on the left page and the information about the great white shark is on the right. This structure helps you compare and contrast the killer whale and great white shark throughout the book.

Strategy: Compare and Contrast

Focus: As you read, use sticky notes to mark similarities between these two animals.

Pages _____

Respond: What physical similarities do the killer whale and great white shark share? What are their physical differences? Fill in the diagram below.

Killer Whale

Both

Great White Shark

Strategy: Determine Importance

Focus: As you read, use a sticky note to mark one important fact about each animal.

Pages _____

Respond: Record each fact you marked. Tell why you think it is important.

Killer Whale	Great White Shark
Fact:	Fact:
It is important because:	It is important because:

Why I Sneeze, Shiver, Hiccup, and Yawn

Ah! Choo!!

by Melvin Berger

Name _____

Date _____

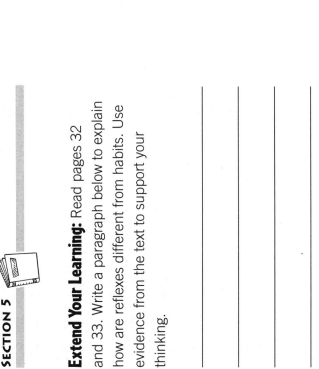

Extend Your Learning: Read pages 32 and 33. Write a paragraph below to explain how are reflexes different from habits. Use evidence from the text to support your thinking.

_____

_____

_____

_____

_____

_____

_____

_____

_____

_____

_____

_____

Strategy: Synthesize

Focus: As you read, use a sticky note to mark a place where you learned something new.

Page _____

Respond: Why are reflexes like shivering and yawning important to the human body?

_____

_____

_____

_____

_____

_____

_____

_____

_____

_____

GET READY TO READ

Strategy: Preview

Think: Have you ever thought about why you sneeze, shiver, hiccup, and yawn? Choose one of these actions, and predict why you think your body does it.

_____

_____

_____

Text Feature Focus: This book includes several diagrams that will help you visualize complex ideas. Turn to page 8. What does the diagram show you? Why do you think the author chose to include a diagram on this page?

_____

_____

_____

_____

READ: Pages 4–13

Strategy: Identify Key Details

Focus: As you read, record the meaning of these important words.

Word	Meaning
reflex	
nervous system	

Respond: What are the two parts of the nervous system?

_____

_____

_____

_____

READ: Pages 14–23

Strategy: Determine Importance

Focus: As you read, use a sticky note to mark three facts.

Pages _____

Respond: Record the three facts you marked in the spaces below. Next, write a star ★ in front of the most important fact, an exclamation point ! in front of the most surprising fact, and a smile ☺ in front of the most interesting fact.

_____

_____

_____

_____

_____

_____

Outside and Inside Sharks

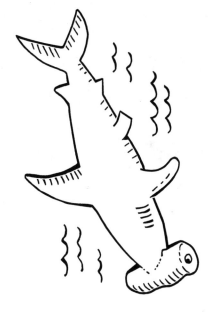

by Sandra Markle

Name _____

Date _____

Extend Your Learning: Use the Glossary on pages 38–39 to create a detailed diagram of a shark's body in the space below or on another sheet of paper. Use as many glossary words as possible for your labels.

READ: Pages 28–37

Strategy: Determine Importance

Focus: As you read, look for important organs found inside sharks. List them:

_____

_____

_____

Respond: In what two ways are young sharks born? What do all baby sharks have in common?

_____

_____

_____

_____

_____

_____

_____

GET READY TO READ

 Strategy: Preview

Think: What do you already know about sharks?

_____

_____

_____

_____

 Text Feature Focus: This book contains many different text features that will help you understand the scientific information presented. It includes photos with captions, diagrams, and a pronunciation guide on page 37. The Glossary at the end of the book will help you understand important vocabulary words.

READ: Pages 3–14

 Strategy: Compare and Contrast

Focus: As you read, record differences between sharks and other types of fish.

Sharks	Other Fish

Respond: How are sharks similar to other types of fish?

_____

_____

_____

_____

_____

_____

READ: Pages 15–27

 **Strategy:** Synthesize

Focus: As you read, look for the different senses sharks use to survive. List the senses you find:

_____

_____

_____

Respond: How do sharks' senses make them the perfect predator?

_____

_____

_____

_____

_____

_____

The Lakota Sioux

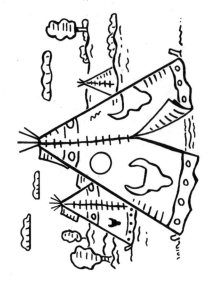

by Andrew Santella

Name _____

Date _____

SECTION 5

Extend Your Learning: Read the words and definitions in the Glossary on page 46. In the space below, create a picture dictionary of the six most important words.

SECTION 4

READ: Pages 28–43

Strategy: Identify Author's Purpose

Focus: As you read, use a sticky note to mark something that surprised you.
Page _____

Respond: Why do you think the author decided to write a book about the Lakota? Use examples from the text to support your opinion.

_____

_____

_____

_____

_____

_____

_____

_____

_____

_____

GET READY TO READ

Strategy: Preview

Think: After previewing the Table of Contents, write a question that came to mind.

_____

_____

_____

Text Feature Focus: This book contains many text features, such as chapter titles, photos with captions, pronunciation keys, maps, and a glossary of important words. These features will help you understand difficult ideas in the text. Before reading each chapter, use the title to help you think about the upcoming information.

_____

_____

_____

_____

READ: Pages 5–13

Strategy: Analyze Cause and Effect

Focus: As you read, record three effects that having horses had on the Lakota people.

1. _____

2. _____

3. _____

Respond: What do you think originally caused the seven groups to form the Seven Council Fires?

_____

_____

_____

_____

_____

READ: Pages 14–27

Strategy: Find the Main Idea

Focus: As you read, record three important details about buffalo in the chart below.

Page	Important Details

Respond: Why was the buffalo so important to the Lakota people?

_____

_____

_____

_____

_____

Snakes

by Seymour Simon

Name _____

Date _____

Extend Your Learning: There are more than 2,500 different kinds of snakes. Which snake would you like to learn more about? Find a book in your classroom or school library, or search the Internet, to help you with your research. Use the following questions to guide you. Jot some notes on the lines. Then, write a report on another sheet of paper.

• Where does the snake live? _____

• What does the snake eat? _____

• What are its natural predators? _____

• How does it protect itself? _____

• How does the snake reproduce? _____

• What are some other interesting facts about the snake? _____

Strategy: Identify Author's Purpose

Focus: As you read, record the characteristics of each type of snake family in the chart below.

Type	Characteristics
Colubridae	
Boidae	
Viperidae	
Elapidae	

Respond: Why do you think the author wrote a book about snakes? Use evidence from the text to support your opinion.

_____

GET READY TO READ

Strategy: Preview

Think: What do you already know about snakes?

_____

_____

_____

_____

_____

Text Feature Focus: This book contains beautiful photos of real snakes from around the world. Previewing the photo on each page before reading will enable you to predict what each section might be about. Since there are no chapter titles or headings, visualizing and mentally summarizing will help you better understand the text.

READ: Pages 4–13

Strategy: Summarize

Focus: As you read, stop at the bottom of each page and think about the most important ideas.

Respond: Summarize the most important ideas on each page listed below.

Page 4	
Page 6	
Page 8	
Page 10	
Page 12	

READ: Pages 14–21

Strategy: Compare and Contrast

Focus: As you read, record how snake and human senses are the same and different.

Same	Different

Respond: How is the reproduction of pythons different from that of boas?

_____

_____

_____

_____

_____

_____

Water Buffalo Days

by Huynh Quang Nhuong

Name _____

Date _____

READ: Pages 87–117

Strategy: Identify Author's Purpose

Focus: As you read, use a sticky note to mark evidence of the author's feelings toward Tank. Page _____

Respond: Based on the last sentence in the book, what do you think the author was saying about war?

_____
_____
_____
_____
_____
_____

Extend Your Learning: Choose three words that best describe Tank's personality. On another sheet of paper, write a paragraph explaining your choices. Use evidence from the text to support your point of view.

READ: Pages 58–86

Strategy: Make Inferences

Focus: As you read, use sticky notes to mark places that reveal Tank's intelligence.
Pages _____

Respond: On page 85, why does the father mention that one thief had been badly hurt in an attempt to steal Tank? Do you think this was the truth or a lie? Use evidence from the text to support your response.

_____
_____
_____
_____
_____

GET READY TO READ

Strategy: Preview

Think: Do you think humans and animals can be best friends? Why or why not?

_____

_____

_____

Text Feature Focus: This book, an autobiography, recounts the author's memories of growing up in Vietnam. Chapter titles will help you focus on the main idea of each chapter. Use the titles and illustrations to support your comprehension as you read each section.

........TIP........

An autobiography is a special type of informational text in which the author tells the story of his or her life.

Strategy: Find the Main Idea

Focus: As you read, use the chapter titles to predict what you will learn about in each chapter. Then use the titles to help you focus on the main idea of each chapter.

Respond: Choose three of the chapters you read. Using the chapter titles to guide you, record the main ideas below.

Chapter Title	Main Idea

Strategy: Summarize

Focus: As you read, stop at the end of each chapter and summarize the most important ideas on a sticky note.

Respond: After reading all three chapters in this section, use your sticky notes to help you write a summary of what you learned.

_____

_____

_____

_____

_____

_____

_____

Exploring the Titanic

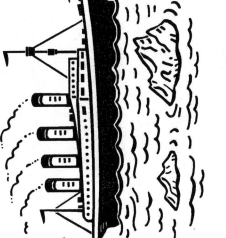

by Robert D. Ballard

Name _____

Date _____

Strategy: Determine Importance

Focus: As you read, use sticky notes to mark places where important discoveries about the wreckage were made by the scientists inside *Alvin*.

Pages _____

Respond: Turn to pages 44 and 45. Use the diagrams to help you record three differences in the *Titanic* before and after it sank.

_____

_____

_____

_____

_____

Extend Your Learning: Refer to the timeline on page 63. On what date did the *Carpathia* arrive in New York City? On another sheet of paper, write an article that could have appeared on the front page of a newspaper that day detailing the *Titanic's* tragic end.

Strategy: Compare and Contrast

Focus: As you read, use a sticky note to mark a place where the author uses a picture comparison to explain an idea.

Page _____

Follow-up: What does the picture show?

_____

_____

Respond: How are *Argo* and SAR similar? How are they different? Refer to pages 30–31 and the Glossary on page 62 to help you complete the chart below.

Same	Different

SECTION 1

GET READY TO READ

Strategy: Preview

Think: What do you already know about the *Titanic*?

Text Feature Focus: This book contains many visual aids, such as photos, diagrams, and maps. It also has a glossary and a timeline. These features will help you understand difficult ideas in the text. Be sure to take your time and use this extra information as you read each section.

READ: Pages 4–9

Strategy: Identify Key Details

Focus: As you read, use sticky notes to mark the names of three people who influenced Robert Ballard's dream of exploring the *Titanic*.
Pages _____

Respond: Using evidence from the text, describe an advance in technology that turned Ballard's dream into a reality.

SECTION 2

READ: Pages 10–17

Strategy: Question

Focus: Chapter Two describes the *Titanic*, the biggest ship in the world in 1912. Write a question you have about the ship.

Follow-up: If your question was answered, use a sticky note to mark the place. Page _____

Respond: Refer to the large diagram of the ship that spans pages 12–15. Why are the rooms divided into first, second, and third class? Use evidence from the text to support your answer.

SECTION 3

READ: Pages 18–29

Strategy: Analyze Cause and Effect

Focus: What caused the *Titanic* to sink?

Use a sticky note to mark where you found the answer. Page _____

Respond: Reread page 24. How did the crew use the lifeboats? Why do you think they did this? What was the result of this decision? Use evidence from the text to support your answer.

How We Crossed the West: The Adventures of Lewis & Clark

by Rosalyn Schanzer

Name _____

Date _____

Extend Your Learning: Choose a person from this book you would like to learn more about. Use the library or Internet resources to read a biography of the person's life. Use the following questions to guide you. Jot some notes on the lines to get started. Then, write a report on another sheet of paper.

• In what era did the person live?

_____

• What were his or her greatest accomplishments?

_____

• What hardships did the person face?

_____

• What important things were happening during the person's lifetime?

_____

• What were some of the person's character traits? How do you know?

_____

READ: Pages 30–41

Strategy: Evaluate

Focus: As you read, use a sticky note to mark evidence of bravery.

Page _____

Respond: What three words do you think the author might use to describe Lewis, Clark, and those who accompanied them on their expedition? Use evidence from the text to support your opinion.

Word	Evidence From the Text	Page

GET READY TO READ

Strategy: Preview

Think: After previewing the book, tell how it is organized.

_____

_____

_____

Text Feature Focus: This book contains many text features, such as maps, illustrations, dates, and headings. The author uses the words of Lewis, Clark, and other party members to tell the amazing true story. As you read, refer to the large map at the beginning of the book to track the expedition.

TIP

Pay attention to the dates placed throughout the book to track the time frame of Lewis and Clark's expedition.

READ: Pages 3–17

Strategy: Make Inferences

Focus: As you read about the beginning part of the journey up the Missouri River, record your inferences in the chart below.

Question?	My Inference
Why did Lewis and Clark choose such a variety of people to bring on the expedition?	
Why did Lewis and Clark give the Native Americans gifts along the way?	
Why were the Arikaras such a healthy looking group of Native Americans?	

Respond: Why was it important for Lewis and Clark to make friends with the Native Americans?

_____

_____

_____

READ: Pages 18–29

Strategy: Summarize

Focus: As you read, record some of the most important ideas in the chart below.

Page	Important Details

Respond: After reading this section write a two- or three-sentence summary of what you learned.

_____

_____

_____

Immigrant Kids

by Russell Freedman

Name _____

Date _____

Extend Your Learning: Imagine you were an immigrant child living in the late 1800s. In the space below, write a short letter to a relative in your home country telling about one part of your new life in America. Use information from the text to make your description more realistic.

READ: Pages 40–67

Strategy: Evaluate

Focus: As you read, use a sticky note to mark something that surprised you.

Page _____

Respond: Do you think children should be allowed to work? Use evidence from the text to support your opinion.

GET READY TO READ

Think: What do you already know about immigration?

_____

_____

_____

_____

Strategy: Preview

Text Feature Focus: This book contains many powerful photos with captions that will help you better understand the time period. Be sure to look carefully at the photos as you read each section.

•••••••••• **TIP** ••••••••••

Take notice of the chapter titles to predict what part of an immigrant child's life will be covered in each chapter.

READ: Pages 1–15

Strategy: Summarize

Focus: As you read, use the 5 Ws to help you record important ideas from the text.

Who? _____

What? _____

When? _____

Where? _____

Why? _____

Respond: Use the information above to help you write a few sentences summarizing what you learned in this section.

_____

_____

_____

_____

_____

_____

READ: Pages 16–39

Strategy: Compare and Contrast

Focus: As you read, look for ways an immigrant child's home life then was similar to and different from your life now.

Similarities	Differences

Respond: How was an immigrant child's school experience different from yours?

_____

_____

_____

_____

_____

What Are Food Chains and Webs?

by Bobbie Kalman

Name _____

Date _____

Extend Your Learning: Choose an activity below to learn more about food chains.

Choice 1: Choose the ecosystem you find most interesting. Make your own food chain and/or web for that ecosystem. Be sure to label your illustrations.

Choice 2: Use what you've learned about food chains and webs to create a public service announcement encouraging others to treat our environment responsibly.

Write some notes on the lines to get started. Then, complete the activity on another sheet of paper.

Notes: _____

_____

_____

_____

_____

_____

_____

READ: Pages 22–29

⭐ **Strategy:** Analyze Cause and Effect

🔍 **Focus:** As you read, look for examples of the effects of the changes in season on food chains and webs. Mark these examples with a sticky note.
Pages _____

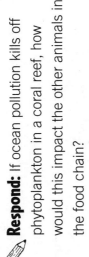 **Respond:** If ocean pollution kills off phytoplankton in a coral reef, how would this impact the other animals in the food chain?

_____

_____

_____

_____

_____

_____

_____

☆ **Strategy:** Preview

💡 **Think:** After previewing the Table of Contents, predict something you will learn from reading this book.

_____

_____

_____

⬇ **Text Feature Focus:** This book is conveniently organized into chapters, which will help you focus on the big ideas in each section. The author also includes many helpful text features, such as pictures with captions, diagrams, headings, subheadings, and bold words. These features will help you understand difficult ideas in the text. Be sure to take your time and use the visual information as you read each section.

☆ **Strategy:** Summarize

🔍 **Focus:** As you read, stop at the end of each section and summarize the most important ideas. Record them below.

What is a food chain?		
Energy from food		
Plants are producers		

✏ **Respond:** How do plants fit into food chains and webs?

_____

_____

_____

_____

_____

_____

☆ **Strategy:** Compare and Contrast

🔍 **Focus:** As you read, look for differences between herbivores, carnivores, and omnivores. Mark these examples with a sticky note.

Pages _____

✏ **Respond:** How are scavengers and decomposers similar? How are they different? Use evidence from the text to help make the comparison.

_____

_____

_____

_____

_____

_____

Duke Ellington

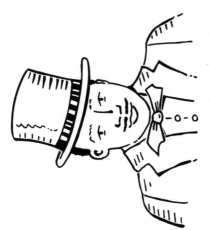

by Mike Venezia

Name _____

Date _____

Extend Your Learning: Review the book for important dates. Use the information to create a pictorial timeline of Duke Ellington's life in the space below.

READ: Pages 22–32

⭐ **Strategy:** Synthesize

🔍 **Focus:** As you read, mark an example of how Duke's experience as an artist, affected his music. Page _____

Explain. _____

✏️ **Respond:** After reading this biography, what lessons can you take from Duke Ellington's life and apply to your own life?

_____

_____

_____

_____

_____

_____

_____

GET READY TO READ

Think: What do you already know about jazz music?

_____

_____

Strategy: Preview

_____

_____

_____

Text Feature Focus: This biography contains many photos and illustrations with captions that support the text.

The sequential order will also aid your comprehension of important life events. Cartoons with speech bubbles are woven throughout the text and give it comic flair.

••••••••••TIP••••••••••

Letters often make more than one sound. On page 8, for example, the *ch* in the word *scholarship* makes the /k/ sound. On page 21, the *que* in the word *unique* also makes the /k/ sound. When trying to figure out a word, zoom in to the tricky part. Then, try out all the different sounds those letters can make until the word make sense.

READ: Pages 3–11

Strategy: Summarize

Focus: As you read, use the 5 Ws to help you record important ideas from the text.

Who? _____

What? _____

When? _____

Where? _____

Why? _____

Respond: Why was "Duke" a fitting nickname for Edward Kennedy Ellington? Use evidence from the text to support your response.

_____

_____

_____

_____

_____

_____

READ: Pages 12–21

Strategy: Make Inferences

Focus: As you read, use sticky notes to mark places that reveal Duke's character through his words or actions.

Pages _____

Respond: Choose a word that describes one of Duke's character traits. Use evidence from the text to support your response.

_____

_____

_____

_____

_____

_____

_____

Harry Houdini: Master of Magic

by **Robert Kraske**

Name _____

Date _____

Extend Your Learning: Choose an activity below to help you think about the information you learned in this book.

Choice 1: Use this biography to create a pictorial timeline of Houdini's life.

Choice 2: Write an essay explaining why you would or would not want to be a magician. Use evidence from the text to explain your point of view.

Write some notes on the lines to get started. Then, complete the activity on another sheet of paper.

Notes: _____

_____

_____

_____

_____

_____

_____

_____

READ: Pages 52–72

⭐ **Strategy:** Evaluate

🔍 **Focus:** As you read, use a sticky note to mark a place that shows something that made Houdini special.

Page _____

✏️ **Respond:** What do you admire about Houdini? Use examples from the text to support your point of view.

_____

_____

_____

_____

_____

_____

_____

Strategy: Preview

Think: After previewing the Table of Contents, write a question that came to mind.

_____

_____

Text Feature Focus: This biography contains some text features, such as chapter titles and photos with captions. Before reading each chapter, use the title to help you think about the upcoming information.

TIP

Some longer words may be difficult to read. Breaking apart these words into syllables will help you sound out the ones you don't know. Try dividing the words below into syllables:

supernatural   congregation

handkerchief

Strategy: Summarize

Focus: As you read, stop at the end of each chapter and summarize the most important ideas on a sticky note.

Respond: After reading these three chapters, use your sticky notes to help you write several sentences summarizing what you learned.

_____

_____

_____

_____

Strategy: Make Inferences

Focus: As you read, use sticky notes to mark places that reveal Houdini's character through his words or actions.

Pages _____

Respond: How do you think Houdini's success in Europe would change his life once returning to the United States?

_____

_____

_____

_____

_____

Kenya

by Jim Bartell

Name _____

Date _____

Extend Your Learning: Read through the Index on page 32 to find a topic to investigate further. Use Internet resources, such as those mentioned on page 31, to help find out more about your chosen topic.

Write some notes on the lines to get started. Then, present your learning orally or through a written project of your choice.

Notes: _____

_____

_____

_____

_____

_____

_____

_____

_____

_____

_____

_____

_____

_____

READ: Pages 20–29

 Strategy: Categorize

Focus: As you read, record important details for each category in the chart below.

Category	Important Details
Entertainment	
Food	
Celebrations	

Respond: Kenyans in different parts of their country eat different kinds of food. How is this similar to the United States?

_____

_____

_____

_____

_____

Reading Response Trifolds for 40 Popular Nonfiction Books Grades 4–6 © 2014 Jennifer Cerra-Johansson Scholastic Teaching Resources • page 49

Strategy: Preview

Think: Locate Kenya on the world map on page 5 in your book. What do you already know about Kenya?

Text Feature Focus: This book is organized into chapters and has many text features, such as a table of contents, photos with captions, bold vocabulary with a corresponding glossary, pronunciation keys, graphs, and maps. The author also includes "fun fact" boxes and "Did you know?" sections to highlight interesting and important information.

Strategy: Summarize

Focus: As you read, stop every few pages and record the most important idea on a sticky note using the prompt:

This was mostly about. . . .

Respond: Use your sticky notes to help you write a brief summary of what you learned about Kenya in this section.

Strategy: Compare and Contrast

Focus: Use sticky notes to mark how your life is similar to and different from that of a child in Kenya.

Pages _____

Respond: How are lives of Kenyans living in the countryside and city similar? How are they different?

Similarities

Differences

Owen & Mzee

by Isabella Hatkoff,
Craig Hatkoff,
and Dr. Paula Kahumbu

Name _____

Date _____

Extend Your Learning: Both Owen and Mzee are extraordinary animals. Choose one of the animals to research. Find a book in your classroom or school library, or search the Internet, to help you with your research. Use the following questions to guide you. Jot some notes on the lines. Then, write a report on another sheet of paper.

• What is the animal's habitat?

_____

• What is the animal's food source?

_____

• What are the animal's predators?

_____

• What are some of the animal's behaviors?

_____

• What are some of the animal's special adaptations?

_____

• How long is the animal's life expectancy?

_____

READ: Pages 25–33

Strategy: Identify Author's Purpose

Focus: As you read this section, use a sticky note to mark a sentence that explains why the authors wrote this book. Page _____

Respond: Why did the authors write this story? How do you know? Use a direct quote from the text to support your opinion.

_____
_____
_____
_____
_____

Strategy: Preview

Think: Think about the word *friendship*. Why does the subtitle describe this friendship as "remarkable"?

_____

_____

_____

Text Feature Focus: This book contains many photos with captions that help this story of friendship come to life. Be sure to examine each photo and read each caption. The authors also included a pronunciation guide after the title page to help with non-English words in the text.

_____

_____

_____

_____

_____

Strategy: Use Context Clues

Focus: As you read, use context clues to determine each word's meaning.

Page	Word	I think it means . . .
8	wallowed	_____
11	surging	_____
12	commotion	_____
14	sanctuary	_____
14	fend	_____

Respond: Was it difficult to rescue the baby hippo? Use evidence from the text to support your answer.

_____

_____

_____

Strategy: Find the Main Idea

Focus: As you read this section, use sticky notes to mark places that demonstrate Owen and Mzee's friendship. Pages _____

Respond: What is the main idea of this section? Use a direct quote from the text to support your answer.

_____

_____

_____

_____

_____

_____

The Top of the World

by Steve Jenkins

Name _____

Date _____

Extend Your Learning: Many books have been written about climbing Mount Everest. Use the library to find another book on this topic. As you read the other book, think about the questions below. After you read the book, respond to the questions.

• What new information did you learn?

_____
_____
_____
_____

• Did you find any information that conflicted with the first book?

_____
_____
_____
_____

READ: Pages 22–32

Strategy: Evaluate

Focus: As you read, list the four main dangers climbers face when hiking Mount Everest.

1. _____

2. _____

3. _____

4. _____

Respond: After reading this book, do you think climbers are brave or foolish to attempt climbing Mount Everest? Use examples from the text to support your opinion.

_____
_____
_____
_____

☆

Strategy: Preview

Think: Would you ever want to climb to the top of a mountain? Why or why not?

_____

_____

_____

_____

_____

⬇ **Text Feature Focus:** This book contains many text features, such as illustrations, diagrams, captions, bold headings, and maps. These features will help you understand difficult ideas in the text. Be sure to take your time and use the visual information to help you read each section.

_____

_____

_____

_____

_____

☆

Strategy: Summarize

Focus: As you read, think about these 5 Ws (and an H) to help you remember important ideas from the text.

How tall is Mount Everest?

Where is Mount Everest?

When were the Himalayan Mountains formed?

What do climbers do when they arrive in Nepal?

Who helps the climbers?

Why did climber George Mallory decide to climb Mount Everest?

✎ **Respond:** Use the information you thought about above to write a few sentences summarizing what you read.

_____

_____

_____

_____

_____

☆

Strategy: Find the Main Idea

Focus: As you read, record three important details in the chart below.

Page	Important Details

✎ **Respond:** What is the main idea of this section?

_____

_____

_____

_____

You Wouldn't Want to Be an Egyptian Mummy!

by David Stewart

Name _____

Date _____

SECTION 5

Extend Your Learning: What do you think of the mummification process? Do you think mummification was a worthwhile endeavor or a waste of time and resources? Write a persuasive essay explaining your point of view. Use evidence from the text to support your opinion.

Write some notes on the lines to get started. Then, complete the activity on another sheet of paper.

Notes: _____

_____

_____

_____

_____

_____

_____

_____

SECTION 4

READ: Pages 22–29

Strategy: Evaluate

Focus: As you read, use a sticky note to mark something that surprised you. Page _____

Respond: Do you think archeologists should remove mummies from their tombs? Explain your thinking.

_____

_____

_____

_____

_____

_____

_____

_____

Strategy: Preview

Think: After previewing the Table of Contents, write a question that came to mind.

_____

_____

Text Feature Focus: This book contains many text features, such as bold headings, photos with captions and labels, and a glossary. Take a few minutes to preview the words in the Glossary on pages 30 and 31. This text feature will be helpful when you encounter specialized vocabulary words in the reading.

• • • • • • • • • • • • **TIP** • • • • • • • • • • • •

The author wrote the book as if you, the reader, are about to undergo the ancient ritual of mummification. Think about how that may make learning historical information interesting.

Strategy: Summarize

Focus: As you read, stop at the end of each chapter and record the most important ideas on a sticky note.

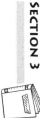

Respond: Use your sticky notes to help you summarize the steps of mummification.

_____

_____

_____

_____

_____

_____

_____

_____

_____

Strategy: Question

Focus: As you read, use a sticky note to mark a place where you thought of a question. Page _____

Record your question: _____

_____

Respond: Why did wealthy Egyptians place *shabtis* in their tombs?

_____

_____

_____

_____

_____

_____

The Discovery of the Americas

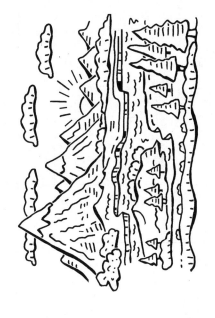

by Betsy and Giulio Maestro

Name _____

Date _____

Extend Your Learning: Read the information on pages 44–45. Choose the ten events you believe are most important. In the space below, create and illustrate a timeline of the events you chose.

Strategy: Evaluate

Focus: As you read, record the most important accomplishment of each explorer mentioned.

Balboa	
Magellan	

Respond: Which explorer do you think made the most important contribution? Use evidence from the text to support your point of view.

_____

_____

_____

_____

GET READY TO READ

☆ **Strategy:** Preview

💡 **Think:** Who do you think discovered America?

_____

_____

_____

🡇 **Text Feature Focus:** This book contains many illustrations and maps that support the text. Be sure to take your time and use the visual information as you read each section.

• • • • • • • • • • **TIP** • • • • • • • • • •

Refer to the Table of Dates on pages 44–45 for a timeline of the history of North America.

READ: Pages 3–17

☆ **Strategy:** Summarize

🔍 **Focus:** As you read, stop every few pages and record the most important idea on a sticky note using the prompt:

This was mostly about. . . .

✏️ **Respond:** Use your sticky notes to help you write a brief summary of what you learned in this section.

_____

_____

_____

_____

_____

_____

_____

_____

READ: Pages 18–33

☆ **Strategy:** Analyze Cause and Effect

🔍 **Focus:** Use a sticky note to mark what caused Europeans to seek alternate trade routes to China. Page _____

Explain. _____

_____

_____

✏️ **Respond:** What effect did Christopher Columbus's discovery have on Europe? Use evidence from the text to support your answer.

_____

_____

_____

_____

_____

_____

_____

Do Tornadoes Really Twist?

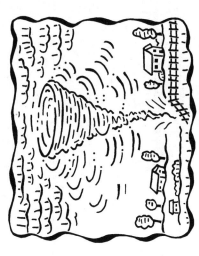

by Melvin and Gilda Berger

Name _____

Date _____

SECTION 5

READ: Pages 38–46

 Strategy: Synthesize

 Focus: As you read, use a sticky note to mark the season when most hurricanes occur. Page _____

Season: _____

 Respond: What do meteorologists and hurricane hunters do? How does their work help people protect themselves from hurricanes?

_____

_____

_____

_____

_____

_____

Extend Your Learning: On another sheet of paper, create a public service announcement or poster telling people how to protect themselves from either a hurricane or tornado.

SECTION 4

READ: Pages 24–37

Strategy: Compare and Contrast

Focus: As you read, use a sticky note to mark an example of how hurricanes and tornadoes are similar. Page _____

Explain. _____

_____

_____

Respond: How do hurricanes and tornadoes cause damage differently?

_____

_____

_____

_____

_____

_____

GET READY TO READ

Strategy: Preview

Think: What do you already know about tornadoes and hurricanes?

_____

_____

_____

_____

⬇ **Text Feature Focus:** Throughout this book, you will find a variety of text features to help you better understand the text. Be sure to carefully read the bold headings, captions, and maps before reading the text on each page. Referring back to the maps during and after reading will also support your understanding.

READ: Pages 3–11

Strategy: Summarize

Focus: As you read, stop at the bottom of each page and write a one-sentence summary on a sticky note.

Respond: What are tornadoes and why do they form?

_____

_____

_____

_____

_____

_____

_____

_____

READ: Pages 12–23

Strategy: Find the Main Idea

Focus: As you read, use a sticky note to mark where in the world most tornadoes form. Page _____

Explain. _____

Respond: How can you protect yourself from a tornado if you are inside? What can you do if you are outside?

_____

_____

_____

_____

_____

_____

Eureka! It's Television!

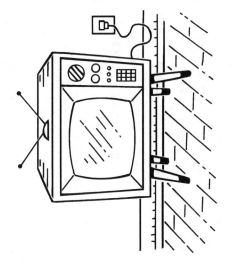

by Jeanne Bendick and Robert Bendick

Name _____

Date _____

Extend Your Learning: Choose an activity below to help you think about the information you learned in this book. Refer to the Index on pages 47–48.

Choice 1: Choose an inventor you would like to learn more about. Use the library or Internet resources to help you with your research. Write a report about this inventor.

Choice 2: Refer to page 45. Back when this book was written, in 1993, these were the advancements inventors were working on. Use the library or Internet resources to find out if any of these inventions came to be. Write a report about these advancements.

Write some notes on the lines to get started. Then, complete the activity on another sheet of paper.

Notes: _____

_____

_____

_____

_____

READ: Pages 30–45

Strategy: Evaluate

Focus: As you read, use a sticky note to mark a place that shows something surprising. Page _____

Respond: What do you think the authors are trying to show about inventions? Use evidence from the text to support your opinion.

Strategy: Preview

Think: After previewing the Glossary on page 46, write a question that came to mind.

_____

_____

Text Feature Focus: This book contains complex scientific information. The diagrams, timelines, and captions will help you understand the difficult ideas in the text. Before reading each page, preview the pictures and refer back to them as needed.

● ● ● ● ● ● ● ● ● ● **TIP** ● ● ● ● ● ● ● ● ● ●

Turn to page 4, the copyright page. Notice that this book was written in 1993. Do you think that fact will have any effect on the information?

Strategy: Find the Main Idea

Focus: As you read, record three important details in the chart below.

Page	Important Details

Respond: What is the main idea of this section?

_____

_____

_____

_____

Strategy: Analyze Cause and Effect

Focus: As you read, use the timeline on pages 24–29 to help you track the inventions that contributed to the creation of the television.

Respond: Choose one of the inventors mentioned in this section. Explain how his invention contributed to the creation of the television.

_____

_____

_____

_____

In the Line of Fire: Eight Women War Spies

by George Sullivan

Name _____

Date _____

SECTION 5

READ: Pages 81–116

 Strategy: Summarize

 **Focus:** As you read, stop every few pages and record the most important idea on a sticky note using the prompt: *This was mostly about . . . .*

Respond: Use your sticky notes to help you write a brief summary of one of the chapters.

_____

_____

_____

_____

Extend Your Learning: Do you think spying is ever justified? Explain why or why not using evidence from the text to support your opinion. Write your response on another sheet of paper.

SECTION 4

READ: Pages 62–80

Strategy: Analyze Cause and Effect

Focus: As you read Chapter 5, mark an event that changed the course of Margareta Zelle's life.

Page _____

Explain. _____

_____

_____

Respond: How did the Kuehn family's spying influence America's involvement in World War II?

_____

_____

_____

_____

_____

GET READY TO READ

 Strategy: Preview

 Think: After previewing the Table of Contents, write a question that came to mind.

_____

_____

➤ **Text Feature Focus:** This book is divided into eight chapters with each chapter focusing on one female spy. The chapter titles and photos with captions will provide some text support. Before reading each chapter, use the title to make predictions and ask questions about the topic.

●●●●●●●●●● **TIP** ●●●●●●●●●●

This book describes the lives of women spies. Think about why the author chose to write only about women.

READ: Pages 1–34

Strategy: Compare and Contrast

 Focus: As you read, use sticky notes to mark evidence of each woman's character. Record words that describe each woman in the chart below.

Lydia Darragh	Rose Greenhow

Respond: How were these two women alike? How were they different?

_____

_____

_____

_____

_____

_____

_____

READ: Pages 35–61

Strategy: Evaluate

 Focus: As you read Chapter 3, use a sticky note to mark a place that shows bravery. Page _____

Respond: Do you think Emma Edmonds was brave or foolish? Use evidence from the text to justify your opinion.

_____

_____

_____

_____

_____

_____

_____

The Story of the White House

by Kate Waters

Name _____

Date _____

Extend Your Learning: Look at the White House portraits on pages 36–38. Choose a President you would like to learn more about. Find resources in the library or on the Internet to help you do your research. Use the following questions to guide you. Jot some notes on the lines. Then, write your report on another sheet of paper.

- During which years did this president serve? _____

- What were some of this president's greatest accomplishments and challenges?

_____

_____

- What were some of this president's character traits? How do you know?

_____

_____

- What important things were happening in the country at the time?

_____

_____

READ: Pages 26–38

Strategy: Evaluate

Focus: As you read, use a sticky note to mark the most interesting fact you learned. Page _____

Respond: Do you think the President and his family should live in such a special house as the White House? Why or why not?

_____

_____

_____

_____

_____

Strategy: Preview

Think: What do you already know about the White House?

_____

_____

_____

➦ **Text Feature Focus:** This book contains many text features, such as photos with captions, illustrations, and maps. These features will help you understand difficult ideas in the text. Be sure to take your time and use the visual information to help you navigate each section.

••••••••• TIP •••••••••

Turn to page 40, the copyright page. Notice that this book was written in 1991. Do you think that fact will have any effect on the information?

_____

_____

_____

_____

Strategy: Summarize

Focus: As you read, think about these 5 Ws (and an H) to help you remember important ideas from the text.

When was the White House built?

Who was the first president to live in the White House?

Where was the White House built?

What happened to the White House in 1812?

Why did they paint it white?

How does the White House represent our country?

Respond: Use the information you thought about above to write a few sentences summarizing what you read.

_____

_____

_____

_____

_____

Strategy: Compare and Contrast

Focus: As you read, use a sticky note to mark something surprising or interesting. Page _____

Respond: How are all of the rooms in the White House similar? How are they different?

_____

_____

_____

_____

_____

The Tarantula in My Purse

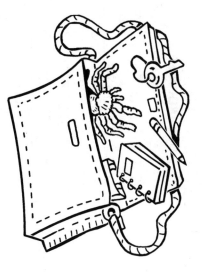

by Jean Craighead George

Name _____

Date _____

Extend Your Learning: Choose an animal from this book you might like to have as a pet. Use the library and Internet resources to learn more about this animal and its way of life. Use the following questions to guide you. Jot some notes on the lines. Then, write a report on another sheet of paper.

• Where does the animal live? _____

• What does it eat? _____

• What are its predators? _____

• What are some of its interesting habits and behaviors?
_____
_____

• What do you know about its young?
_____
_____

• What other interesting facts did you discover?
_____
_____

READ: Pages 88–134

Strategy: Identify Author's Purpose

Focus: As you read, use a sticky note to mark a place that made you feel an emotion strongly. Page _____

Describe your feeling. _____
_____
_____

Respond: Why do you think the author decided to share these stories? What was she trying to teach the reader? Use evidence from the text to support your opinion.
_____
_____
_____
_____
_____
_____

★ **Strategy:** Preview

💡 **Think:** Do you think people should keep wild animals as pets? Why or why not?

_____

_____

_____

_____

↘ **Text Feature Focus:** This book contains 21 true stories about the various wild animals the author had as pets while raising her three children. Each chapter includes a title, which will enable you to make predictions and ask questions about the topic before reading. Information about the animals is woven throughout the stories, so you need to think about each story's moral as well as the scientific information acquired while reading.

★ **Strategy:** Categorize

🔍 **Focus:** As you read, think about what is scientific information and what is a deeper life lesson.

✏️ **Respond:** Use the chart to record the scientific information and the life lessons you learned.

Scientific Information	Life Lesson

★ **Strategy:** Synthesize

🔍 **Focus:** As you read, use sticky notes to mark places where the author's pets interact with each other.

Pages _____

✏️ **Respond:** Were you surprised by any of the interactions the animals had with each other? Explain. Use evidence from the text to support your response.

_____

_____

_____

_____

_____

_____

Colonial Times From A to Z

by Bobbie Kalman

Name _____

Date _____

Extend Your Learning: Read the words and definitions in the Glossary on page 32. In the space below, create a picture dictionary of the six most important words.

READ: Pages 21–31

Strategy: Evaluate

Focus: As you read, use a sticky note to mark a place that describes something you would not like about colonial life.

Page _____

Respond: Do you think all Americans should learn about colonial history? Why or why not?

_____

_____

_____

_____

_____

_____

_____

_____

_____

Strategy: Preview

Think: After previewing the Table of Contents, write a question you think might be answered from reading this book.

_____

_____

Text Feature Focus: This ABC book contains many photos and illustrations with captions. Preview the pictures on each page before reading to help you make predictions and ask questions about the topic.

•••••••••• **TIP** ••••••••••

Some longer words may be difficult to read. Breaking apart these words into syllables will help you sound out the ones you don't know.

Strategy: Categorize

Focus: As you read, record the topics you learn about under the correct category below.

Clothing	Survival	Children

Respond: How is categorizing information helpful when reading nonfiction?

_____

_____

_____

Strategy: Compare and Contrast

Focus: As you read, use a sticky note to mark a similarity between your life and the colonists'. Page ____

Explain. ____

Respond: What is the biggest difference between colonial life and your life? Use evidence from the text to support your response.

_____

_____

_____

SECTION 4

READ: Pages 56–72

☆ **Strategy:** Question

🔍 **Focus:** As you read, use a sticky note to mark a place where you thought of a question. Page _____

Record your question: _____

✏️ **Respond:** Why do you think Levi's jeans have been so successful for such a long period of time?

SECTION 5

Extend Your Learning: Of all the inventions you read about, which one do you think had the biggest effect on humans? Jot some notes on the lines to get started. Then, on another sheet of paper, describe the invention and write a persuasive essay about it. Use evidence from the text to support your opinion.

Notes: _____

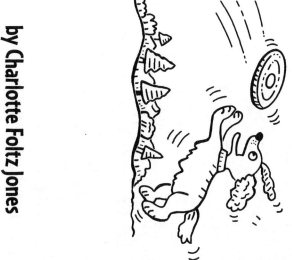

Mistakes That Worked

by Charlotte Foltz Jones

Name _____

Date _____

GET READY TO READ

Strategy: Preview

Think: After previewing the book, read the Introduction. What do you think the author wants you to learn from reading this book?

_____

_____

_____

_____

 **Text Feature Focus:** The author has categorized the inventions into chapters with an overall theme. This will help you make connections and better understand the text. The fun illustrations on each page also support the text. At the back of the book, an index will enable you to find inventions quickly if you need to refer back to inventions you already read about.

READ: Pages 1–34

Strategy: Analyze Cause and Effect

Focus: As you read Chapter 1, use a sticky note to mark an example of cause and effect. Page _____

Respond: Choose an invention from Chapter 2. Tell what caused the creation of the invention, and explain what effect the invention has had on people.

Invention: _____

_____

Cause: _____

_____

_____

Effect: _____

_____

_____

READ: Pages 35–55

Strategy: Determine Importance

Focus: As you read, use a sticky note to mark three facts.

Pages _____

Respond: Record the three facts you marked in the spaces below. Next, write a star ★ in front of the most important fact, an exclamation point **!** in front of the most surprising fact, and a smile ☺ in front of the most interesting fact.

_____

_____

_____

_____

_____

_____

_____

_____

SECTION 4

READ: Pages 22–32

Strategy: Identify Author's Purpose

Focus: As you read, use a sticky note to mark a place that shows something surprising. Page _____

Respond: Why do you think the author wants people to learn more about penguins? Use examples from the text to support your opinion.

_____

_____

_____

_____

_____

_____

_____

_____

_____

_____

SECTION 5

Extend Your Learning: Choose a type of penguin found in this book. Use the library and Internet resources to find out more information about this type of penguin. After finishing your research, create your own informational book about the penguin you studied. Use the following questions to guide you. Jot some notes on the lines to get started.

• Where does this penguin live? _____

• What does it eat? _____

• What are its predators? _____

• How does it care for its young? _____

• What are some of its characteristics and behaviors? _____

_____

_____

Penguins! Strange and Wonderful

by Laurence Pringle

Name _____

Date _____

SECTION 1

GET READY TO READ

Strategy: Preview

Think: Write a question that came to mind as you previewed this book.

_____

_____

Text Feature Focus: This book contains a map and many illustrations with labels showing the various types of penguins. These features will help you understand difficult ideas in the text. Be sure to take your time and use the visual information as you read each section. Preview the illustrations before reading the text on each page.

• • • • • • TIP • • • • • •

When trying to sound out tricky words such as _Humboldt_, dividing the word between two consonants will make it easier to pronounce.

SECTION 2

READ: Pages 3–11

Strategy: Compare and Contrast

Focus: As you read, use a sticky note to mark the things all penguins have in common. Page _____

Respond: What are the six groups of penguins? Choose two of the six groups to compare and contrast.

1. _____
2. _____
3. _____
4. _____
5. _____
6. _____

Two Groups: _____

Similarities	Differences

SECTION 3

READ: Pages 12–21

Strategy: Summarize

Focus: As you read, stop every few pages and record the most important idea on a sticky note using the prompt: _This was mostly about . . . ._

Respond: After reading, use your sticky notes to help you write a brief summary of what you learned in this section.

_____

_____

_____

_____

_____

_____

_____

_____

_____

_____

SECTION 4

READ: Pages 44–63

⭐ **Strategy:** Compare and Contrast

🔍 **Focus:** As you read, record three differences between a pioneer family and your family.

1. _____

2. _____

3. _____

✏️ **Respond:** How are pioneer mothers similar to and different from mothers of today?

_____

_____

_____

_____

_____

_____

SECTION 5

READ: Pages 64–87

⭐ **Strategy:** Summarize

🔍 **Focus:** As you read, stop at the end of each section and summarize the most important ideas on a sticky note.

✏️ **Respond:** Use your sticky notes to help you write a brief summary of what you learned.

_____

_____

_____

_____

_____

_____

_____

Extend Your Learning: Imagine you were a pioneer heading west in the 1800s. On another sheet of paper, write a letter to a relative back home to describe life in your new surroundings. Refer to examples in the text to make your letter more realistic.

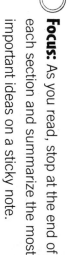

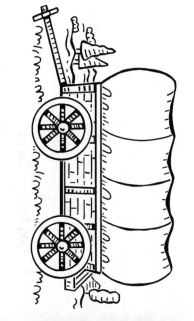

Pioneers

by Martin W. Sandler

Name _____

Date _____

SECTION 3

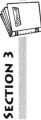

READ: Pages 26–43

Strategy: Analyze Cause and Effect

Focus: As you read, list the new means of transportation that were invented in the pioneer era.

_____

_____

Respond: Which method of transportation had the greatest effect on westward expansion? Use evidence from the text to support your response.

_____

_____

_____

_____

_____

_____

_____

_____

SECTION 2

READ: Pages 4–25

Strategy: Find the Main Idea

Focus: As you read, use the bold headings and photos to predict what you will learn about. Then use them to help you focus on the main idea of each section.

Respond: What motivated most pioneers to make the dangerous journey out west?

_____

_____

_____

_____

_____

_____

_____

_____

SECTION 1

GET READY TO READ

Strategy: Preview

Think: What do you already know about pioneers and westward expansion?

_____

_____

_____

 Text Feature Focus: This book contains many visual sources from the Library of Congress. Text features, such as photos, illustrations, and maps, will help you understand difficult ideas in the text. Be sure to take your time and use the visual information as you read each section.

SECTION 4

READ: Pages 26–37

☆ **Strategy:** Analyze Cause and Effect

🔍 **Focus:** As you read, record three effects the volcano had on the surrounding area.

Effect 1: _____

Effect 2: _____

Effect 3: _____

✏️ **Respond:** How did the arrival of colonizers impact the area devastated by the eruption?

_____
_____
_____
_____
_____
_____
_____
_____

SECTION 5

READ: Pages 38–58

☆ **Strategy:** Identify Author's Purpose

🔍 **Focus:** As you read, use sticky notes to mark evidence of the author's purpose.

Pages _____

✏️ **Respond:** What do you think the author wanted you to learn from reading this book?

_____
_____
_____
_____
_____

Extend Your Learning: This book was about the volcano Mount St. Helens. Use the library or Internet resources to find out about another volcano. Then, on another sheet of paper, write a report about the volcano. How is it similar to and different from Mount St. Helens?

Volcano

by Patricia Lauber

Name _____

Date _____

SECTION 3

READ: Pages 8–25

⭐ **Strategy:** Use Context Clues

🔍 **Focus:** As you read, use context clues to determine each word's meaning.

Page	Word	I think it means . . .
9	avalanche	_____
9	magma	_____
14	pumice	_____
16	crater	_____

✏️ **Respond:** What is the difference between magma and lava?

_____

_____

_____

_____

_____

_____

_____

_____

SECTION 2

READ: Pages 1–7

⭐ **Strategy:** Summarize

🔍 **Focus:** As you read, use the 5 Ws to help you record important ideas from the text.

Who? _____

What? _____

When? _____

Where? _____

Why? _____

✏️ **Respond:** Use the information above to help you write a brief summary of this section.

_____

_____

_____

_____

_____

_____

SECTION 1

GET READY TO READ

⭐ **Strategy:** Preview

💡 **Think:** After previewing the Table of Contents, write a question you think might be answered in this book.

_____

_____

➔ **Text Feature Focus:** This book contains many text features, such as photos, diagrams, captions, and maps. These features will help you understand difficult ideas in the text. Be sure to take your time and use the visual information as you read each section.

• • • • • • • • • • **TIP** • • • • • • • • • •

When sounding out a long word, look for smaller words inside of it.

SECTION 4   READ: Pages 90–140

⭐ **Strategy:** Find the Main Idea

🔍 **Focus:** As you read, use the chapter titles to predict what you will learn about in each chapter. Then use the titles to help you focus on the main idea of each chapter.

✏️ **Respond:** After reading, record the main idea of each chapter. Use the chapter titles to help you.

Chapter Titles	Main Idea

SECTION 5   READ: 141–188

⭐ **Strategy:** Analyze Cause and Effect

🔍 **Focus:** Use a sticky note to mark an effect of the bus boycott.

Page _____

✏️ **Respond:** What were some of the laws passed as a result of the civil rights movement? How did these laws help African Americans?

_____

_____

_____

_____

_____

_____

Extend Your Learning: Choose three words that best describe Rosa Parks's character. On another sheet of paper, write an essay explaining your choices. Use evidence from the text to support your point of view.

Rosa Parks: My Story

**by Rosa Parks
With Jim Haskins**

Name _____

Date _____

SECTION 1

GET READY TO READ

 Strategy: Preview

Think: What do you already know about Rosa Parks?

_____

 Text Feature Focus: This book, an autobiography, is organized into chapters with titles. The titles will help you focus on the main idea of each chapter. Some photos with captions are spread throughout the book to help you visualize important people and events.

● ● ● ● ● ● ● ● ● **TIP** ● ● ● ● ● ● ● ● ●

When sounding out a long word, try going past the vowel and scooping up the consonant in order to break the word into syllables.

SECTION 2

READ: Pages 1–54

 Strategy: Identify Author's Purpose

 Focus: As you read, stop at the end of each chapter and summarize the most important ideas on a sticky note.

 Respond: Why do you think Rosa Parks devoted the first three chapters providing background information about her childhood? Use evidence from the text to support your response.

_____
_____
_____
_____
_____
_____
_____

SECTION 3

READ: Pages 55–89

Strategy: Make Inferences

Focus: As you read, use sticky notes to mark places that reveal Raymond Parks's character through his words or actions. Pages _____

Respond: Why did Rosa Parks and her husband fight to help African Americans even though it was dangerous? What does this show about their character?

_____
_____
_____
_____
_____
_____
_____

SECTION 4

READ: Pages 54–80

Strategy: Find the Main Idea

Focus: As you read, use the headings to predict what you will learn about in each section. Then use the headings to help you focus on the main idea.

Respond: Explain the headings for each section below. How do they help you determine the main idea?

Heading	Explanation
Hairy Mats and Hissing Fits	
Tarantula Frontiers	
"Elle Est Belle, Le Monstre"	

SECTION 5

Extend Your Learning: Read through the references on page 79. Choose another species to investigate. Use Internet resources, such as those the author provided, to help you learn more. Before beginning your research, write a list of questions you would like to answer.

My Questions:

1. _____

2. _____

3. _____

4. _____

5. _____

6. _____

The Tarantula Scientist

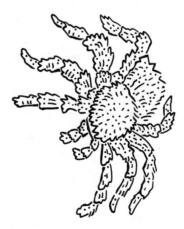

by Sy Montgomery

Name _____

Date _____

SECTION 1

GET READY TO READ

 Strategy: Preview

Think: What do you already know about spiders?

_____

 Text Feature Focus: This book contains many text features, such as photos with captions, maps, and headings. Use the headings to make predictions and ask questions about the topic. This will help you focus on important information in the text.

• • • • • TIP • • • • •

Many nonfiction books have an index. An index appears in alphabetical order and helps you know where to find specific information in a book. In this book, you can find it on page 80. On what page(s) would you learn about . . .

● grooming behaviors? _____ _____

● molting? _____ _____

● venom? _____ _____

SECTION 2

READ: Pages 6–29

 Strategy: Summarize

Focus: As you read, think about these 5 Ws (and an H) to help you remember important ideas from the text.

Where is Sam studying tarantulas?

Who is the "Queen of the Jungle"?

What do tarantulas do to protect themselves?

When did tarantulas first appear on Earth?

How do tarantulas eat their prey?

Why is Sam in the jungle looking at tarantulas?

Respond: Use the information you thought about above to write a few sentences summarizing what you read.

_____
_____
_____
_____
_____

SECTION 3

READ: Pages 30–53

Strategy: Identify Key Details

Focus: As you read, record three important details about tarantulas in the chart below.

Page	Important Details

Respond: How do most spiders use their silk?

_____
_____
_____

SECTION 4

READ: Pages 86–123

☆ **Strategy:** Evaluate

🔍 **Focus:** As you read, use a sticky note to mark a place that shows something about Obama's character.

Page ____

✏️ **Respond:** What qualities does Obama possess that make him an effective politician? Use evidence from the text to support your opinion.

_____
_____
_____
_____
_____
_____
_____
_____
_____
_____

SECTION 5

Extend Your Learning: If you had a chance to speak with Obama, what would you say? What questions would you ask? Record them on the lines below. On another sheet of paper, write a letter to President Obama expressing your thoughts.

My Questions:

1. _____

2. _____

3. _____

4. _____

5. _____

6. _____

Barack Obama

by Stephen Krensky

Name _____

Date _____

SECTION 3

Strategy: Find the Main Idea

Focus: As you read, use the chapter titles to predict what you will learn about in each chapter. Then use the titles to help you focus on the main idea.

Respond: Choose one of the chapters you read. Write the chapter's main idea. Then record three details that support the main idea.

Main Idea: _____

_____

Detail 1: _____

_____

Detail 2: _____

_____

Detail 3: _____

_____

SECTION 2

Strategy: Analyze Cause and Effect

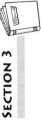

Focus: As you read, use sticky notes to mark important experiences from Obama's childhood and adolescence. Pages _____

Respond: Choose an experience you marked. Explain what effect(s) it had on Obama's life and his future.

_____

_____

_____

_____

_____

_____

SECTION 1

Strategy: Preview

Think: After previewing the Table of Contents, write a question that came to mind.

_____

_____

_____

Text Feature Focus: This biography contains many helpful text features, such as a table of contents, index, vocabulary text boxes, photos with captions, maps, and bold chapter headings. These features will help you understand difficult ideas in the text. Be sure to take your time and use the visual information as you read each section.

SECTION 4

READ: Pages 92–132

☆ **Strategy:** Make Inferences

🔍 **Focus:** As you read, use sticky notes to mark places that reveal Lincoln's character through his words or actions.

Pages _____

✏️ **Respond:** On page 130, the author ends the chapter with a direct quote from a newspaper clipping that was found in Lincoln's pocket. Why do you think the author chose to end the book with this particular quote?

_____

_____

_____

_____

_____

_____

_____

_____

_____

_____

_____

SECTION 5

Extend Your Learning: Pages 133–137 include quotes from Lincoln's letters, speeches, and personal discussions. Choose the quote you feel is most powerful and copy it below. On another sheet of paper, explain what the quote shows about Lincoln's character.

_____

_____

_____

_____

_____

_____

_____

_____

_____

_____

_____

Lincoln: A Photobiography

by Russell Freedman

Name _____

Date _____

READ: Pages 44–91

Strategy: Find the Main Idea

Focus: As you read, use sticky notes to mark two important events that inspired Lincoln to pursue politics.

Pages _____

Respond: What events led Lincoln to emancipate the slaves? Use evidence from the text to support your response.

_____
_____
_____
_____
_____
_____
_____
_____
_____

READ: Pages 1–43

Strategy: Summarize

Focus: As you read, use sticky notes to mark important ideas in each chapter.

Pages _____

Respond: After reading, use the sticky notes to help you write a one-sentence summary for each chapter.

Chapter 1	**Chapter 2**	**Chapter 3**

GET READY TO READ

Strategy: Preview

Think: After previewing the Table of Contents, describe something you might learn about Abraham Lincoln from reading this book.

_____

Text Feature Focus: This book contains many photos and letters with captions that support the main text. In addition, the author organized the book into chapters that each begin with one of many of Lincoln's quotes. Use the chapter titles and quotes to help you make predictions and ask questions before reading. This will help you focus on the "big idea" in each chapter.

SECTION 4

READ: Pages 100–138

Strategy: Make Inferences

Focus: As you read, use sticky notes to mark places where people's emotions are revealed through their actions.

Pages _____

Respond: What lessons can be learned from reading about the Great Chicago Fire of 1871?

_____

_____

_____

_____

_____

_____

_____

_____

_____

SECTION 5

Extend Your Learning: Choose an activity below to help you think about the information you learned in this book.

Choice 1: Explore ways the Great Chicago Fire changed Chicago forever. What were the negative effects? What were the positive effects? Find resources in the library or on the Internet to help you do your research. Write a report to share with your class.

Choice 2: Author Jim Murphy has written other accounts of historical disasters such as *Blizzard!* Choose another book by this author to help you complete an author study. After reading the book, write an essay to compare and contrast the book you chose with *The Great Fire.*

Write some notes on the lines to get started. Then, complete the activity on another sheet of paper.

Notes:

_____

_____

_____

_____

The Great Fire

by Jim Murphy

Name _____

Date _____

SECTION 1

GET READY TO READ

Strategy: Preview

 **Think:** After previewing the Table of Contents, predict something you will learn from reading this book.

_____

  Text Feature Focus: This book contains many text features, such as photos and illustrations with captions, maps, and chapter titles. These features will help you understand difficult ideas in the text. The author uses first person accounts of the disaster to help him tell the story. Keeping track of the many people involved can be difficult. Be sure to visualize and reread any parts where you encounter confusion.

SECTION 2

READ: Pages 11–42

Strategy: Analyze Cause and Effect

Focus: As you read, use sticky notes to mark places that explain what caused the fire to spread so easily.
Pages _____

Respond: How did human error play a role in causing the great fire to spread?

_____
_____
_____
_____
_____
_____
_____
_____

SECTION 3

READ: Pages 43–99

Strategy: Evaluate

Focus: As you read, use sticky notes to mark places where the author clearly conveys the feelings of those involved in the disaster.
Pages _____

Respond: How does this author help readers "experience" the disaster without actually being in Chicago during the fire? What emotions did you feel while reading this section?

_____
_____
_____
_____
_____
_____
_____
_____

SECTION 4

READ: Pages 22–31

⭐ **Strategy:** Identify Author's Purpose

🔍 **Focus:** As you read, use a sticky note to mark something that surprised you.

Page _____

✏️ **Respond:** Why do you think the author wanted to tell this story? What do you know about the way the Cannon-Street All Stars were treated? Explain.

_____

_____

_____

_____

_____

_____

_____

_____

SECTION 5

Extend Your Learning: Jackie Robinson was the first African American to play baseball in the major leagues. Read a biography about his experience. How was it similar to that of the Cannon-Street players?

Write some notes on the lines to get started. Then, on another sheet of paper, write an essay comparing and contrasting the experiences.

Notes: _____

_____

_____

_____

_____

_____

_____

_____

Let Them Play

by Margot Theis Raven

Name _____

Date _____

Strategy: Make Inferences

Focus: As you read, use a sticky note to mark evidence of prejudice.

Page _____

Respond: Why do you think the Cannon-Street All Stars made the long trip to Pennsylvania even though they weren't guaranteed to play? Use evidence from the text to support your response.

Strategy: Summarize

Focus: As you read, think about these 5 Ws (and an H) to help you remember important ideas from the text.

When does this story take place?

Where does this story take place?

Who was involved?

What did they want?

Why was this important?

How did the parents support the players?

Respond: Use the information you thought about above to help you write a few sentences summarizing what you read.

Strategy: Preview

Think: What do you already know about segregation?

 Text Feature Focus: This book tells the true story of a little league team that fought for fairness during segregation in the South. It is told in narrative form so it reads more like a story than an informational book. As you read, be sure to think about the most significant events to help you follow the ideas in the story.

SECTION 4

READ: Pages 55–77

⭐ **Strategy:** Identify Author's Purpose

🔍 **Focus:** As you read, use a sticky note to mark a place where Stanton's actions reveal her character.

Page _____

Follow-up: What does the picture show?

✏️ **Respond:** Why do you think the author decided to write a book about Elizabeth Cady Stanton? Use evidence from the text to support your opinion.

_____

_____

_____

_____

_____

_____

SECTION 5

Extend Your Learning: Use the library and Internet resources to learn more about women's suffrage. Create a timeline in the space below highlighting the most important events that led to the 19th Amendment.

You Want Women to Vote, Lizzie Stanton?

by Jean Fritz

Name _____

Date _____

GET READY TO READ

Strategy: Preview

Think: What do you already know about women's suffrage?

_____

Text Feature Focus: This book about Elizabeth Cady Stanton's life also serves as a timeline about the women's suffrage movement. The eight chapters are told sequentially to help readers track Stanton's important life events as well as significant moments that eventually led to women gaining the right to vote.

• • • • • • • • • • **TIP** • • • • • • • • • •

Some longer words may be difficult to read. Breaking apart these words into syllables will help you sound out the ones you don't know.

Strategy: Analyze Cause and Effect

Focus: As you read, use sticky notes to mark events that influenced Stanton and caused her to act on behalf of women. Pages _____

Respond: What effect did meeting Lucretia Mott have on the course of Stanton's life?

_____
_____
_____
_____
_____
_____
_____

Strategy: Find the Main Idea

Focus: As you read each chapter, think about the "big ideas." Create an appropriate title for each chapter that speaks to the most important ideas.

Chapter 4	
Chapter 5	
Chapter 6	

Respond: What recurring challenges did Stanton face throughout this section?

_____
_____
_____
_____

SECTION 4

READ:

Strategy: _____

Focus: _____

Respond: _____

_____

_____

_____

_____

_____

_____

_____

_____

_____

_____

_____

_____

SECTION 5

Extend Your Learning: _____

_____

_____

_____

_____

_____

_____

_____

_____

_____

_____

_____

_____

Title: _____

Author: _____

Name _____

Date _____

READ: _____

⭐ **Strategy:** _____

🔍 **Focus:** _____

✏️ **Respond:** _____

READ: _____

⭐ **Strategy:** _____

🔍 **Focus:** _____

✏️ **Respond:** _____

GET READY TO READ _____

⭐ **Strategy:** _____

💡 **Think:** _____

➡️ **Text Feature Focus:** _____

Bibliography

Barack Obama by Stephen Krensky (DK Publishing, 2010)

Cats vs. Dogs by Elizabeth Carney (National Geographic Society, 2011)

Colonial Times From A to Z by Bobbie Kalman (Crabtree, 1997)

Constellations by Diane M. Sipiera and Paul P. Sipiera (Children's Press, 1997)

The Discovery of the Americas by Betsy and Giulio Maestro (Scholastic Education edition, 1992)*

Do Tornadoes Really Twist? by Melvin and Gilda Berger (Scholastic, 2000)

Duke Ellington by Mike Venezia (Children's Press, 1995)

Endangered Animals by Lynn M. Stone (Scholastic, 1984)

Eureka! It's Television! by Jeanne Bendick and Robert Bendick (Scholastic Education edition, 1993)*

Exploring the Titanic by Robert D. Ballard (Scholastic/Madison Press, 1988)

The Great Fire by Jim Murphy (Scholastic, 1995)

Harry Houdini: A Master of Magic by Robert Kraske (Scholastic Education edition, 1973)*

Heroes of the Revolution by David A. Adler (Scholastic Education edition, 2004)*

How We Crossed the West: The Adventures of Lewis & Clark by Rosalyn Schanzer (National Geographic Society, 1997)

Immigrant Kids by Russell Freedman (Penguin, 1980)

In the Line of Fire: Eight Women War Spies by George Sullivan (Scholastic, 1996)

Kenya by Jim Bartell (Bellwethermedia, 2011)

The Lakota Sioux by Andrew Santella (Children's Press, 2001)

Let Them Play by Margot Theis Raven (Sleeping Bear Press, 2005)

Lincoln: A Photobiography by Russell Freedman (Scholastic Education edition, 1988)*

Mistakes That Worked by Charlotte Foltz Jones (Delacorte Press, 1991)

Outside and Inside Sharks by Sandra Markle (Aladdin, 1996)

Owen & Mzee by Isabella Hatkoff, Craig Hatkoff, and Dr. Paula Kahumbu (Scholastic, 2006)

Penguins! Strange and Wonderful by Laurence Pringle (Boyds Mills Press, 2007)

Pioneers by Martin W. Sandler (Eagle, 1994)

Rocks and Minerals by Ann O. Squire (Children's Press, 2002)

Rosa Parks: My Story by Rosa Parks With Jim Haskins (Scholastic Education edition, 1994)*

Snakes by Seymour Simon (HarperCollins, 1992)

Stargazers by Gail Gibbons (Holiday House, 1992)

The Story of the White House by Kate Waters (Scholastic, 1991)

The Tarantula in My Purse by Jean Craighead George (HarperCollins, 1996)

The Tarantula Scientist by Sy Montgomery (Houghton Mifflin, 2004)

The Top of the World by Steve Jenkins (Houghton Mifflin, 1999)

Volcano by Patricia Lauber (Bradbury Press, 1986)

Water Buffalo Days by Huynh Quang Nhuong (HarperCollins, 1997)

What Are Food Chains and Webs? by Bobbie Kalman (Crabtree, 1998)

Who Would Win? Killer Whale vs. Great White Shark by Jerry Pallotta (Scholastic, 2009)

Why I Sneeze, Shiver, Hiccup, and Yawn by Melvin Berger (Scholastic Education edition, 2000)*

You Want Women to Vote, Lizzie Stanton? by Jean Fritz (Putnam, 1995)

You Wouldn't Want to Be an Egyptian Mummy! by David Stewart (Scholastic, 2001)

* Scholastic Education editions by arrangement with original publisher